PROJECT ECO-CITY

Your Living Home
Your Wild Neighbourhood
Town Life
Global Cities

This book was prepared for Wayland (Publishers) Ltd by
Globe Education, Nantwich, Cheshire

Concept design and artwork by SPL Design

Cover picture: A house mouse

First published in 1994 by
Wayland (Publishers) Ltd
61 Western Road, Hove
East Sussex, BN3 1JD, England

Printed and bound by
G. Canale & C. S. p. A., Turin

British Library Cataloguing in Publication Data
Parker, Philip
Your Living Home. — (Project
Eco-city Series)
I. Title II. Series
574.5268

ISBN 0 7502 1304 3

Picture acknowledgements:
Biophoto Associates 5l, 7b, 9t, 11
Bruce Coleman 28 (Kim Taylor)
Ecoscene 26t, 26b, 29 (Robin Williams), 36 (Robin Williams), 38, 39, 41l, 41r, 42t, 44t (Paul Thompson),
45b (Sally Morgan)
Heather Angel *cover*, 4, 12b, 14, 42b, 45t
NHPA 5tr (Michael Leach), 5br (Stephen Dalton), 12t (Stephen Dalton), 13 (Stephen Dalton), 16 (Stephen Dalton),
17t (Stephen Dalton), 24t (Walter Murray), 24b (David Woodfall), 25t (J. J. Soothill), 25b (Stephen Dalton),
32 (Stephen Dalton), 40 (Ken Griffiths), 43 (Michael Leach), 44b (Stephen Dalton)
Oxford Scientific Films 6, 8t, 9b, 10, 15 (Harold Taylor), 17b (Jim Frazier), 19b (Avril Ramage), 20 (Larry Crowhurst),
21 (John Downer), 22, 31 (David Thompson), 34 (Barrie Watts), 35 (J. A. L. Cooke)
Science Photo Library 7m (P. Hawtin, University of Southampton), 8b (Andrew Syred),
18 (Dr Tony Brain & David Parker) 19t (Jane Shemilt, Cosine Graphics), 37 (Biophoto Associates)
Zefa 7t

Contents

A unique habitat

If you are interested in plants and animals you don't have to make a special expedition to the country, or even to the zoo. You will find a fantastic zoo of your own much closer to home. We share our town with huge numbers of plants, birds, mammals, reptiles and especially insects. Many have changed, or adapted, to suit city life, and some creatures couldn't survive without towns. They live well in the surroundings, or environment, of a city just as other wildlife survive in other environments, such as forests or rivers.

In the UK, there are around 15 million gardens covering almost half a million hectares, and most of these have dozens of different plants, from trees and shrubs to flowers and weeds. The plants provide food and shelter for a wealth of animals, which are in turn eaten by other creatures. But you don't even need to go outside to find some of the most fascinating wildlife.

How many living things are there in your home? There are people and perhaps pets, but there will also be hundreds of different types, or species of animals giving birth, feeding, reproducing and dying right in your home. Most never go outside; some are happy raiding your larder, other animals eat those who do the raiding! But you don't even have to stir out of bed to find wildlife – they will find you!

For as long as humans have lived in towns they have tried to control house mice – 6,000 year old mouse traps have been found in ancient houses in Afghanistan!

Roof roosters — long-eared bats at rest in a house attic. When flying, their ears are almost as long as their bodies.

As your home is your own shelter, your body is home to dozens of species of tiny life forms. The moisture, warmth and food our bodies provide make it an ideal home to millions of tiny life forms inside and on us. Most are so small that they can only be seen through a microscope.

Ecology is the special study of how living things affect, and are affected by, their environment. This book looks at the ecology of our gardens, yards, homes... and our bodies.

▲ Your body is teaming with bacteria, or germs, which can only be seen through powerful microscopes.

Wherever there are humans, there are houseflies eager to feast on leftovers. ▶

On or under your skin

You don't have to look very far to find wildlife. Look no further than your own body – we carry around with us a fantastic zoo of living things.

All living things are made up of tiny cells. All the important chemistry that keeps living things alive happens in cells. You are made up of many millions of cells, but simple life forms are made up of just one. The bacteria are a group of single-celled living things. They are so small you need a microscope to see them – a teaspoon would hold more than 150,000 million bacteria.

You are home to thousands of millions of bacteria. Draw a square 1 cm by 1 cm on your skin and you will have drawn a line around 5 million bacteria. Bacteria also like your insides where it is dark, warm, wet and there is plenty of food. Having so many bacteria is perfectly normal and healthy, but some bacteria can make you ill. Your body has special defences to control them. Your stomach makes a very strong acid and the tears from your eyes contain chemicals to keep the bacteria from increasing their numbers. Unwanted bacteria in your body are 'sensed' by your cells and special chemicals are sent to find the bacteria and kill them. You also have white blood cells which can 'swallow' up bacteria.

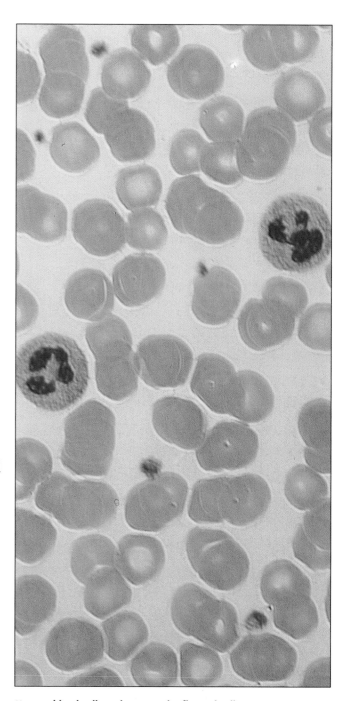

Human blood cells – these are the flat red cells carry oxygen around your body. The white blood cells defend you against germs.

White blood cells are very good at swallowing bacteria, but not the other tiny lodgers in your body. These are viruses which are even smaller than bacteria. They are a strange group of living things; they don't have a cell 'body' themselves, but need to enter the cell of a living thing before they can start to grow. They can live inside a cell without causing trouble, but when 'woken' a virus begins to reproduce and can damage, or even kill, the cell. A cold sore is one example of the effect of a virus. Fortunately your body has some good defences. Antibodies are chemicals made in your blood and they can attach themselves to the invading viruses and kill them.

Coughing and sneezing are part of having a common cold.

The adenovirus is one cause of the common cold. It is only one ten-thousandths of a millimetre wide.

DID YOU KNOW?

Bountiful bacteria

You have around 100,000 million bacteria living on your skin, but millions more inside your body. Life would be impossible without them. For example, some help you digest your food; others turn milk into butter, cheese and yogurt; some bacteria help make the soil fertile so food plants can grow. Scientists can make both bacteria and viruses into vaccines. These can be put into your body, usually by an injection, and will help to protect you against diseases.

In your gut live millions of these bacteria called *E. Coli*. Without them you couldn't digest your food.

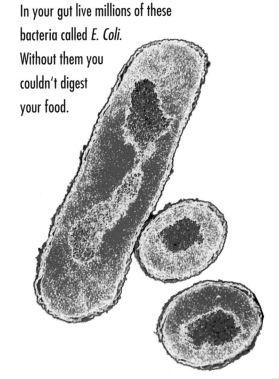

Body creepers

You probably have eight-legged relatives of spiders lurking on you. These are the mites, and they feed on the scales of our skin and dig down to suck up our blood. They are so small that we don't know they are there. At worst, they can burrow deep into the skin and cause a disease called scabies – but this is fairly rare.

The demodex mite is tiny – just 0·3 mm long – and prefers to live head down in the tiny 'pockets' from which your hairs grow. These are called hair follicles, and your eyelashes are favourite haunts of this mite. Just 10 hours after mating, a female will lay her eggs at the root of a follicle. Two days later tiny copies of the adult mites called larvae emerge, except that they have six legs. The hard casing which surrounds them does not grow as their bodies grow, and soon falls off leaving behind eight-legged young mites.

The youngsters are soon washed out of the follicle by the rivers of tears that keep your eyes moist. The mites then wander over the skin until they find a new follicle in which to live. A demodex mite's life lasts just two weeks – and it all happens just above your eyes.

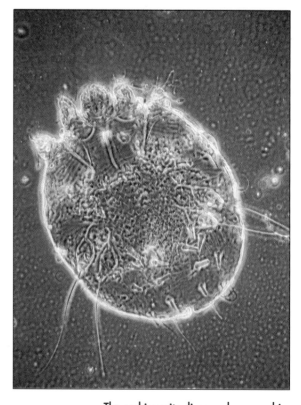

The scabies mite dives under your skin.

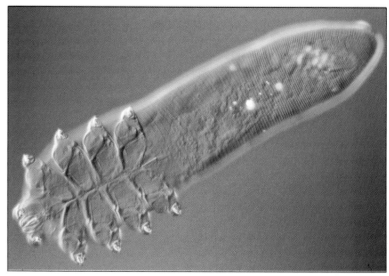

A demodex mite – there are five or six mites living above each of your eyes.

The human body louse — which feeds only on warm blood.

If you are very unlucky you may catch lice. These are wingless insects with flat bodies that are less than 1 mm long – so you have to look very hard to see them. On humans, lice live on hair. They have strong claws that have become adapted to grip a single hair.

Lice lay tiny white eggs, called 'nits', and fix them to the hair of their host with a glue. We can sometimes suffer from lice when lots of people are together, such as in schools. But the lice – and the nits – can be removed by shampoos.

The house dust mite.

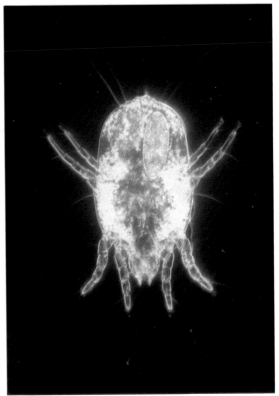

DID YOU KNOW?

There were one million in a bed...
Many kinds of mite live on us, and feed off us. As we walk along, thousands of tiny flakes of skin fall off and we only notice when we see dust (most house dust is made up of skin flakes). Even as you sleep, the flakes still come off. They are so small that they fall through the weave in your pyjamas, through the bed sheet to the gentle 'dust' mites who wait to feast on your waste skin. You probably share your bed with a million of them.

Pets and pests

If you have a dog or cat you probably know that it has to be 'wormed'– given a powder to get rid of troublesome creatures called nematodes – or worms. These are not like earthworms, but tiny animals which are parasites – they live in or on a creature and give nothing back in return for the favour. Puppies are almost always born with worms and are usually wormed before they are sold. But this may not get rid of the eggs.

One species of worm is particularly dangerous to humans. When a female worm has mated, she lays eggs in the gut of the dog. The eggs travel through the gut with the waste material which passes out, perhaps on to the grass of a park. The eggs can survive there for many months, and may be accidentally touched by a human. If the person then touches his or her mouth, the eggs can travel down into the gut. There they grow into larvae before journeying to other parts of the body where they can cause damage – even blindness. Every year in the UK about 100 people have their sight affected by this worm. So, it is important to have puppies wormed regularly, have dogs checked for worms, and for owners to stop dogs leaving their waste in places where people play.

A dog hook worm.

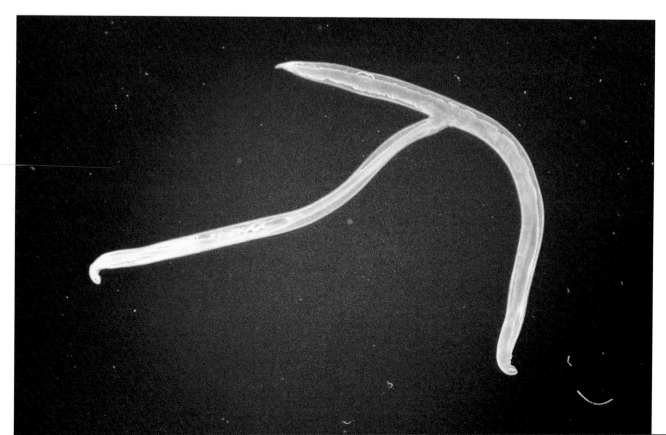

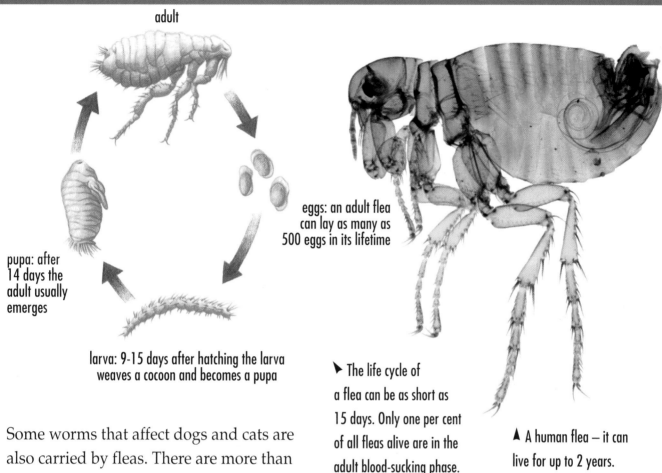

adult

eggs: an adult flea can lay as many as 500 eggs in its lifetime

pupa: after 14 days the adult usually emerges

larva: 9-15 days after hatching the larva weaves a cocoon and becomes a pupa

▶ The life cycle of a flea can be as short as 15 days. Only one per cent of all fleas alive are in the adult blood-sucking phase.

▲ A human flea – it can live for up to 2 years.

Some worms that affect dogs and cats are also carried by fleas. There are more than 1,600 species of flea. Dog fleas prefer dogs; human fleas prefer humans, but they are not too fussy and will live on other creatures. Dog, cat and human fleas are about 2 mm long and can go a whole year without feeding. They have special mouth parts to break the skin and suck blood, and their back legs allow them to make huge jumps. A flea can jump 200 times its own length – for a human to do the same she would have to jump over the Empire State Building in New York!

Spraying, powdering or shampooing your pet will only kill the fleas living on your animal. Hundreds of eggs fall from the host and stick on carpets and furniture. Flea larvae hatch and feed on skin flakes and adult flea droppings. Two weeks after hatching, the larvae weave a sticky covering called a cocoon around them. They have become pupae, and remain like this, covered in carpet hairs and impossible to see, for up to two years, but usually, two weeks. The warmth of a host, like a dog, or even you, awakens the flea. It emerges from the pupa, climbs aboard, and takes its first meal of blood.

Food thieves

A bluebottle laying eggs on fish.

Bluebottle larvae are used by anglers as bait to catch fish.

To see how wildlife has slowly adapted to take advantage of city life, we need look no further than the creatures we think of as pests.

One of the most unwelcome sounds in the home is the whine of the housefly which is made by flapping its wings 20,000 times a second. The blowfly (or bluebottle) is another uninvited guest. Both flies feed with a long coiled tube, called a proboscis. They land on a piece of food and pass chemicals down the proboscis to dissolve it. A soup-like substance is then sucked back up the proboscis into the mouth. The flies feed on bacteria-filled rubbish and manure, and can soon be feeding on human food. So flies spread bacteria – and their hairy bodies can pick up germs, too.

Houseflies lay their eggs in rotting food and manure, while blowflies lay their eggs on dead animals or meat left in the home or in the waste bin. In hot weather, the eggs hatch in less than a day and the wriggly white larvae (or maggots) emerge. It takes just one week for these larvae to develop into adult flies. In hot weather the number of flies in towns increases rapidly and they thrive in the decaying waste and food found in homes and streets.

Unlike flies, cockroaches are hardly affected by the temperature – thanks to the heating systems in our homes. The ancestors of cockroaches lived in hot, tropical countries – so warm houses are not very different for them. Hiding in cracks in bathrooms and kitchens during the day, cockroaches come out at night to raid food stores, and eat woollen clothes and even wallpaper. Although they have small wings, they hardly ever fly – but they are one of the fastest runners in the insect world.

Oriental cockroach eating pasta.

CATCHING AND KEEPING FRUIT FLIES

To make your fly trap, carefully cut a plastic bottle in half as shown below. Place the ripe fruit in the trap and leave by an open window. In warm weather, tiny fruit flies may gather. Collect some of the flies in a jam jar, add some of the fruit, and cover with some muslin or stocking, securing it with a rubber band. Repeat with other jars and keep them in a warm place. Watch the flies and count the days as eggs may be laid and hatch.

What happens? Draw a picture of the life cycle of a fruit fly.

How to make a fruit fly trap.

plastic bottle

cut round with scissors

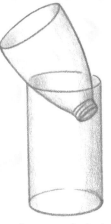

put the top inside the bottom

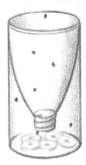

put ripe fruit inside the trap

13

Silverfish and weevils

Silverfish, along with firebrats, are very simple, ancient animals. Creatures like these have been on the Earth for 30 million years. They are wingless insects covered in silvery scales, and with three 'tails', making them look a little like fishes. Firebrats live in warm places and have longer antennae and tails than silverfish, which live in the corners of cupboards and larder shelves. Both feed on sweet or starchy foods and search for flour, sugar, breadcrumbs and even the glue in cardboard boxes or in the binding of books.

The female silverfish lays only 20 eggs in her life. She finds cracks and holes and lays her eggs in them leaving them to hatch. Tiny silverfish emerge and take 6 months to grow to the size of their parents. Like all insects, they grow by shedding their outer casings.

More wingless relatives of the silverfish are the springtails. These can be found in damp cellars but more often in gardens. They are usually brown or grey and have a special way of escaping when in danger. Attached to their undersides is a tiny 'spring', clipped up under their bodies when not in use. When disturbed, the spring is released, flicks down on the ground, and the springtail is thrown through the air to safety.

Weevils feasting on flour. Both adult beetles and their larvae are shown in this picture.

There are thousands of different species of weevil. They are very small, sometimes brightly-coloured beetles, with a long snout at the front of their heads. At the tip of the snout are sharp mouth parts. Weevils are very successful insects, perhaps because of their snouts, which allow them to drill into plants and reach in for food.

The few weevils which live in homes make use of this snout to drill through paper bags to get to the flour and cereals stored inside. If you have weevils, throw away any food they have reached, and never keep flour and cereals in paper bags for longer than a week. Put them in glass or plastic containers.

Silverfish eating a meal.

KEEPING SILVERFISH

Silverfish are no trouble to keep. Look for them in the corners of cupboards, under the paper lining of drawers, under draining boards and in other damp places such as garden sheds. Place a few in a jar with some crumpled moist paper towels.

Make holes in the lid for air. Put silverfish in a warm, dark place and feed them on breadcrumbs. Watch them carefully.

How do they use their antennae? Do they eat anything else in the jar?

Silverfish can be kept like this for up to a year.

A jar for keeping silverfish.

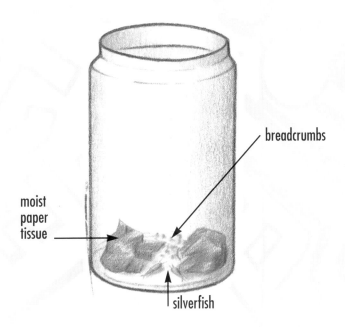

breadcrumbs

moist paper tissue

silverfish

Mice and rats

The name 'house mouse' does not do this mammal justice! It has been found living alongside humans almost everywhere: at the bottom of mine shafts, in dockside warehouses, even inside deep-freezers! Mice have probably been with humans since our ancestors lived in caves.

Mice are rodents – mammals with one pair of sharp gnawing teeth at the top of their mouths. Many house mice will spend the warmer summer months in gardens, yards and fields and only move indoors when the days get cooler.

Sometimes they climb up the spaces behind walls to reach attics, or they gnaw holes through wood and walls to enter kitchens. With the warmth and rich pickings of food in most houses, mice can breed all year long. A female may have as many as 10 litters of young in a year, and each litter will have eight baby mice. For three weeks the babies feed from their mother; by eight weeks they are fully grown and able to breed. It is no wonder that mice have proven impossible to control despite poisons, traps, and cats.

House mice chew anything – even electric cables.

The agile brown rat running along a water pipe.

Like all rodents, rats carry fleas which can feed on human blood. The black rat carried the fleas which spread the Black Death virus throughout Europe and Asia in the 14th century which killed 50 million people. Because it is so good at running along the rafters in attics it has been called the 'roof rat'. Since the black rat prefers to live inside buildings it is easier for people to find and kill. It has also been unable to compete for food with its relative, the brown rat.

The brown can eat a much wider range of food and live in many more places. Brown rats have been known to eat water pipes, electric cables and building timbers and have caused burst pipes and fires. Their sharp teeth grow throughout life, and so the rat needs to gnaw regularly to wear them down. Unlike the black rat, the brown thrives in sewers beneath buildings, and on rubbish dumps.

DID YOU KNOW?

Rat race in the White House
In the summer of 1993 the US President's home, the White House in Washington DC, was invaded by rats. Gardeners set 165 rat traps in the White House grounds, but it made little impact on the hundreds of rats. Perhaps this isn't surprising. Washington was built on a drained swamp, and rats, racoons, possums, snakes and mosquitos have long been a fact of life. At the same time, the Houses of Parliament in London were plagued by mice.

A brown rat with
its new born litter.

Wood-eaters

Imagine hundreds of unwanted guest coming to your home for dinner! This is exactly what they do – at this moment there are probably insects eating your furniture!

Have you ever seen small holes in old wooden furniture, doors and timber frames? These are the entrances to the tunnels bored by woodworms – the larvae of furniture beetles. The larvae of many species of beetle eat their way through trees or rotting wood, but some species have found plenty of wood inside people's houses.

The furniture beetle lays its eggs in cracks on the surface of the wood. Once the larvae emerge from the eggs, they dig tunnels through the wood, eating as they go. For up to five years they burrow along the grain of the wood. Then they turn into a pupa just below the surface, and eventually break through the wood to emerge as adults. The holes we see on the wood are escape holes made by the new adult. At worst, the wood is turned into a crumbling shell of sawdust.

A furniture beetle emerging out of its hole.

Whereas the woodworm makes holes of 1 mm diameter, much bigger holes suggest the presence of the death-watch beetle. The larvae of this beetle prefers to eat oak and is usually found in buildings such as old churches.

Termites are another well-known group of wood-eating insects, although few species cause damage to homes. They are mostly found in hot, tropical countries, but some species live as far north as Maine and Vancouver in North America. Termites eat cellulose, an important material in plants, but they rely on the bacteria in their guts to digest this for them. Some termites tunnel under houses and enter through the wooden floors. Others make nests inside the wood they feed on and are much more difficult to control.

Woodworm tunnels in roof timbers.

Woodworm damage to wooden chair legs. If one piece of furniture has woodworm, all the other wooden furniture in a room may have them within 6 months.

DID YOU KNOW?

Death-watch beetles
The larvae of the death-watch beetle can eat through old timber beams for two or three years. When the adult male emerges he hits his head inside the tunnel where the larvae lived, making a knocking sound. Scientists think he does this to attract a mate. This is probably why the death-watch beetle got its name – the knocking sound would be heard in a quiet church where people were watching over the dead.

Eight-legged hunters

Your home is sought-after by a huge variety of wildlife. It is not only a place of shelter, it provides a good, reliable source of food.

Unlike most of the creatures that live in our homes, spiders are not insects. They belong to a group known as arachnids, which also contains mites. Spiders live almost entirely on living animals, mostly insects. They catch their prey and with their needle-like fangs they bite and inject a poison into it. Then they suck out the body juices. Not all spiders make webs, but all make silk. The silk begins as a liquid which emerges from holes in the underside of the spider. As soon as it reaches the air, the silk turns into a long thread.

Each thread is a rope of many fine threads, each only 0·0003 mm across. The long-legged house spiders make an untidy 'sheet web'. Undisturbed, the web may be up to a metre long. One corner of the web is rolled up to make a tube where the spider waits. Once an insect lands and gets stuck on the web, the spider senses the vibrations and rushes out to kill its prey.

Most spiders have several eyes, but despite this they cannot see very well. They rely on the bristles on their bodies and legs to pick up the vibrations on the web. A spider can immediately tell what creature has become entangled from the vibrations it makes.

A house spider with prey caught in its web.

Look for spiders in corners and cracks in walls, among plants, and in garden sheds. A temporary home can be made from a jar with a paper lid which has air holes pierced in it. Put some damp soil inside and a roll of paper for the spider to climb on.

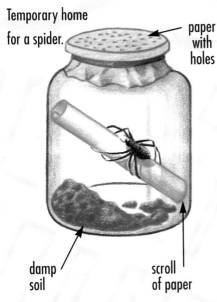

Temporary home for a spider.

paper with holes

damp soil

scroll of paper

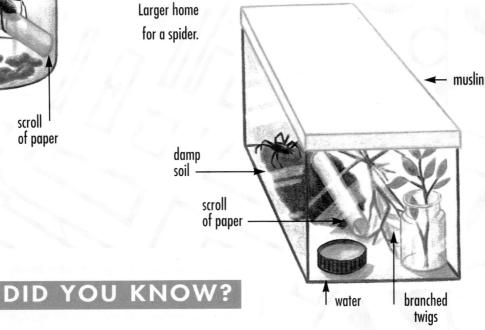

Larger home for a spider.

muslin

damp soil

scroll of paper

water

branched twigs

DID YOU KNOW?

Spider facts

The spiders you share your house with are the most useful lodgers you could wish for. They pay their rent through the insects they catch. Scientists have calculated that in one year the spiders in England and Wales eat a weight of insects the same as the weight of all the people who live there! A house spider can live for up to seven years.

If you want the spider to spin a web, put it in a larger home. Use a small aquarium with a muslin top and include some water and twigs. Keep the aquarium out of sunlight and don't keep the spiders for more than a few days.

Up against the wall

Even in the most desolate concrete backyard there will be living things busy changing the environment, and making it a more welcoming place for life. They are the real gardeners!

Like cliff faces, walls are not easy places for life to thrive. But they are usually full of life. Scientists investigating different walls in UK cities found at least 185 different species on them. And the older wall, the more life there will be.

Dandelions growing on a brick wall in the middle of town.

A new wall is as barren as the surface of the moon and the first things to colonize it are simple plants. The green slime that often coats damp walls is algae. This lush pasture is grazed by snails, woodlice, millipedes and some caterpillars. Lichens and mosses will hug the wall in patches of cushions, trapping moisture and helping the plant to survive dry periods. Lichens are two plants in one. An algae makes the food, while a fungus creates the acid which eats into the stone and anchors the whole plant to the wall. This partnership of two life forms in one is called symbiosis.

Field poppies growing on an old stone wall.

Lichens are the pioneers. Their roots dig away at the wall, and they sometimes make a weak acid which dissolves the mortar. Then more complex plants can grow, such as rosebay willowherb, or fireweed. Since each rosebay can make 80,000 seeds per summer to be spread by the wind, it is no wonder that the plant we think of as a weed will spread rapidly.

Crevices provide homes for animals, and plants give food and shelter to small creatures like springtails and beetles, which are hunted by spiders, mice and birds. When a wall is covered by ivy, honeysuckle and other flowering plants there will be nectar for moths and flies. An old wall can even support a large yew or elm tree.

INVESTIGATE THE ECOLOGY OF A WALL

Find an old wall and look for pioneering plants such as slimy algae, lichens, mosses and ferns. What flowering plants can you find? What eats the plants?

Use a magnifying glass to explore small crevices and look under leaves. Is there a difference between the life at the bottom and top of the wall?

ivy

lichen

moss

woodlouse

nettle

buddleia

snail

Aphids and ants

Aphids are tiny bugs that feed on plants – have you seen them in your backyard or garden? With their tiny needle-like teeth they bite into plants to drink the juices, damaging the plant. They also carry viruses which interfere with the plant's growth. The green plants make food with the help of the energy from the sun, which the aphids feed on. The aphids are in turn eaten by ladybirds and lacewings. If it were not for these insects, aphid numbers would rise rapidly. The movement of energy from sun to plant to aphid and then ladybird is an example of a food chain.

Another insect which seeks out aphids, but for a different reason is the black ant. Ants particularly like sweet foods and even enter houses in search of them. Sometimes they are seen climbing trees and bushes to feed upon the sticky honeydew which oozes from aphids. They 'milk' the aphids of their honeydew; the aphids are not harmed by this. Some ants even carry aphid larvae to their nest, caring for them over the cold winter months, and returning them to their trees in the spring.

Ants live in large groups, or colonies, headed by one or more queen ants. A queen may live for ten years, hidden away underground, perhaps under a garden path. Here she lays her eggs and looks after them. Soon larvae hatch and within a few weeks small 'worker' ants emerge which set about excavating the passages and chambers of the new nest.

Ant 'milking' aphids for honeydew.

The ants bring food for the queen who lays more eggs, which the workers then take to special chambers where they hatch into larvae and are fed. Finally, new male and queen ants develop. Unlike the workers, they have wings, and when the weather and temperature is just right, the workers allow them out of the nest for the first time for their 'marriage flight'. Huge swarms of them can be seen on summer days. Most are eaten by birds, but some manage to mate, and the queens are ready to find a new nest and begin the cycle again.

A red ant tending larvae in the nest.

EXAMINE THE WAY ANTS LIVE

Look for ants under stones in a garden or yard and collect some. Put some moist soil in a large jar and stand it in a dish or basin of water (to stop the ants escaping). Put the ants in the jar and cover the top with a piece of plywood or thick card which has a hole in the middle.

Put some honey on a small piece of bark and place it on the cover along with some cake crumbs. Cover the ant house with a box to keep the light out and after a few days check the ants. Have they started to tunnel? Replace the box, and check the ants again after a few days.

Return the ants to where you found them when you have finished.

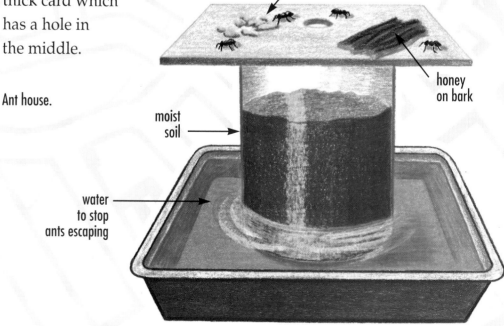

Ant house.

cake crumbs

honey on bark

moist soil

water to stop ants escaping

Worms

Under your feet in your garden or backyard is a thriving world of life. The soil contains huge numbers of living things, from tiny roundworms, or nematodes, to moles. The nematodes are related to those that can live in a dog or cat – but exist in much bigger numbers. Mark out an area of one metre by one metre on the soil and you have drawn a line around 20 million nematodes. Most nematodes are less than one millimetre long – many can only be seen with a microscope – but they are everywhere: in soil, living things, and water.

Nematodes are made up of one segment, and are very different from earthworms which can have up to 250 segments.

Each segment has four pairs of tiny bristles, and by using these and their muscles, earthworms push their way between the particles of soil as they burrow. They are some of the most useful animals in the garden. Their tunnelling mixes up the soil and allows air to flow to plant roots, which encourages the decay of material and the release of minerals into the soil.

Worms also burrow by swallowing the soil in front of them. The waste soil is pushed back behind them towards the surface. Rainwater tends to wash the minerals out of surface soil to the lower layers, so the worms' eating habits put the best soil back towards the plants.

How worms burrow
down through soil.

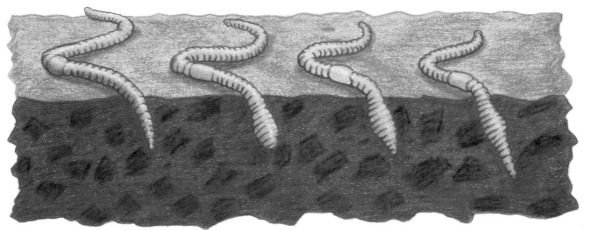

| worm anchors its rear end with bristles and pushes its front end into the soil | front becomes fatter as more segments squeeze in behind | the muscles contract | front end becomes long and thin again pushing further into the soil |

A mole eats up to 50 worms a day.

Some gardens may also have a mole. It spends almost all its life underground, eating mostly worms and slugs. With its powerful front legs and long claws it excavates tunnels and piles soil up on the surface in 'mole hills'. Its fur lies in two directions, so if it gets into trouble it can easily reverse through its tight-fitting tunnel.

WORMING AROUND

Make a simple wormery from a large jar or drink bottle. Slightly moisten some garden soil and some compost bought from a gardening shop. Make alternate layers of soil and compost and add a few worms to the surface with some leaves. Roll a sheet of black paper around the outside of the jar to keep out the light, and put the wormery outside. Occasionally lift the black paper to see the soil layers. What happens to the layers?

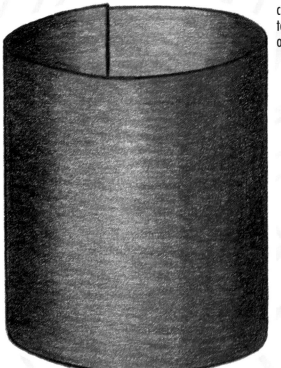

cover to slide over jar

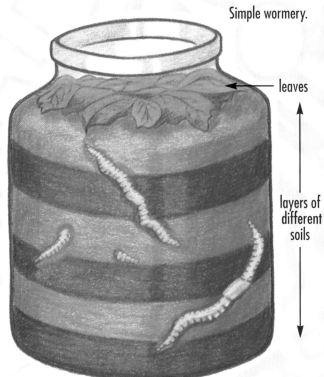

Simple wormery.

leaves

layers of different soils

Look – no legs!

Some garden creatures don't have a waterproof covering and so are always in danger of drying out. This is why many come out at night, or shelter under stones and leaves during the day.

To escape the sun and dryness of the air during the day, slugs burrow into the soil, and snails shut themselves up in their shells and seal the entrance with a waterproof door of mucus. A snail's shell grows all the time, and is mostly made of chalk. This is why snails prefer to live on soils which have chalky chemicals. Those few snails that are found on acid soils (which have little chalk) will usually have very thin shells.

You may find dozens of species of snail in a garden. Although they can live up to ten years, they have many enemies, particularly thrushes which have learnt how to crack open their shells. Holding the shell in its beak, the thrush brings it down hard on a favourite sharp stone. Once the shell is off, the thrush wipes the snail on the ground to remove most of the sticky mucus which could gum up its beak.

Slugs are snails without shells, although some species have a small oval shell just under the skin. Like snails, slugs have two pairs of stalks, or tentacles, on their heads. The longer pair have eyes, the shorter pair can smell things. Slugs eat almost anything they can find, including garden plants, but mostly they eat leaves and dead plant material. Those slugs with hidden shells eat earthworms, and burrow into the soil in search of them.

The snail has thousands of tiny teeth on its tongue, which shred food so it may be eaten. Next time you see a snail feeding – listen closely!

A home for snails.

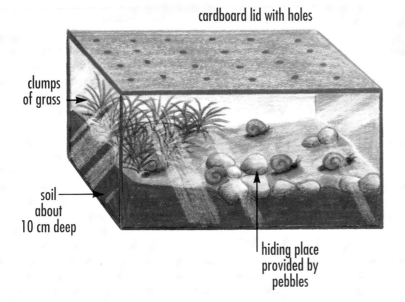

cardboard lid with holes

clumps of grass

soil about 10 cm deep

hiding place provided by pebbles

Put a depth of 10 cm of soil in an aquarium, add some stones for hiding places and plant a few clumps of grass. Place some snails in the aquarium and cover with a lid of cardboard with holes bored in it. Feed the snails on fresh cabbage and lettuce and remove old food.

Watch how the snail moves and climbs. Slime pours out of a special opening on its underside and the animal 'swims' along on this. The slime is also sticky, allowing it to climb up walls and even glass.

A snail's obstacle course.

A snail climbing the side of a jar.

Watch how the snail climbs inside a jar. Muscles ripple along the body, lifting each part in turn, 'wafting' the body forward on the slime. Look for light and dark bands – the light ones are the parts that are not moving.

Release the snails in the garden when you have finished studying them.

Fourteen legs

Probably every garden has woodlice hiding from the sun under logs, stones and dead leaves. They are not insects, but belong to a group of animals called crustaceans, which also includes crabs. Although their ancestors lived in water, they do not have a waterproof skin, and so they prefer to live in damp places and feed at night. Woodlice have a rotten diet – they mostly eat dead and decaying plants. In turn they are eaten by shrews, toads, beetles and some spiders.

Summer is the woodlouse breeding season. The female has a 'pouch' on her underside into which she lays her eggs. A month later the eggs hatch and tiny woodlice emerge – each the size of a grain of rice. After a few days about 25 youngsters emerge.

The hard outer covering of a woodlouse cannot grow, so the woodlouse sheds this skin from time to time to grow a bigger one. The new covering is soft and white but soon hardens and darkens in colour. If you find a black and white woodlouse it is halfway through growing a new coat. After two years, the woodlice can breed, and will live for perhaps another two years.

One species of woodlouse can roll itself up into a tight ball when frightened. Look for pill bugs along the base of garden walls where the mortar provides the lime needed for its thick coat. In the past these woodlice were swallowed by people who believed they could calm upset stomachs – this is probably why they have the name 'pill bugs'.

During the breeding season, female woodlice grow a pouch on their undersides into which they lay their eggs. It takes a month for the eggs to hatch and young to emerge.

A woodlouse is covered by hard plates which overlap rather like the tiles on a roof.

Into a clean container put some damp soil, moss (to keep the soil wet), pieces of rock and rotting wood, and some chalk and potato. Add a few woodlice and cover the container with paper with breathing holes. Keep in a shady place and clean out every two weeks. Why do you need to add the chalk?

Experiments with light and damp

Put a thin strip of damp blotting paper in one half of a tray and cover that half with a card. Do the same in another tray but this time cover the dry half.

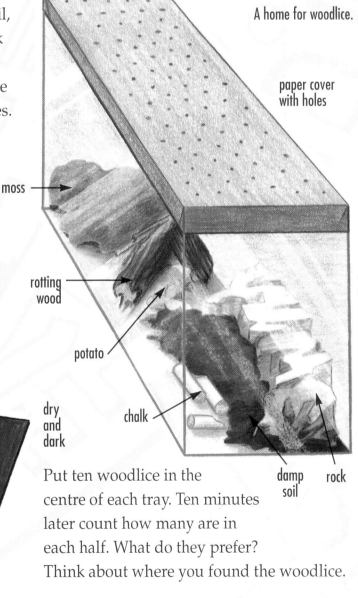

A home for woodlice.

paper cover with holes

moss

rotting wood

potato

chalk

damp soil

rock

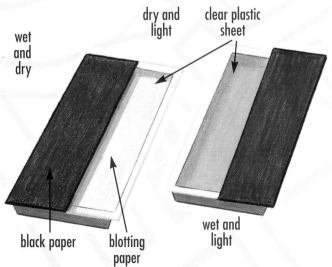

wet and dry

dry and light

clear plastic sheet

dry and dark

black paper

blotting paper

wet and light

Put ten woodlice in the centre of each tray. Ten minutes later count how many are in each half. What do they prefer? Think about where you found the woodlice.

Not one thousand legs!

Dig in the garden and you may soon find a flat, red-brown, many-legged creature – the centipede. Its body is made up of segments, and it is a ferocious carnivore (a meat eater). It hunts slugs and insects and so is useful in the garden. The word 'centipede' means 100 feet, but the real number varies from species to species – as few as 34 or as many as 254 feet. Most centipedes are small, less than 10 mm long, but are fast movers. The first pair of legs are not used for walking; they have poison fangs to kill their prey.

Centipedes come out at night to avoid the sun. Very few species have eyes; they rely on their sense of touch and on the special smelling cells in their long antennae. Centipedes lay eggs one at a time and special claws at the rear of their bodies handle the eggs and smear them with a sticky liquid.

▲ A centipede in search of woodlice, spiders, beetles, springtails and other prey.

◄ It is not easy to tell the difference between a centipede and a millipede. Look carefully at the segments in the middle of each body. Centipedes have two legs on each segment while millipedes have four.

centipede

millipede

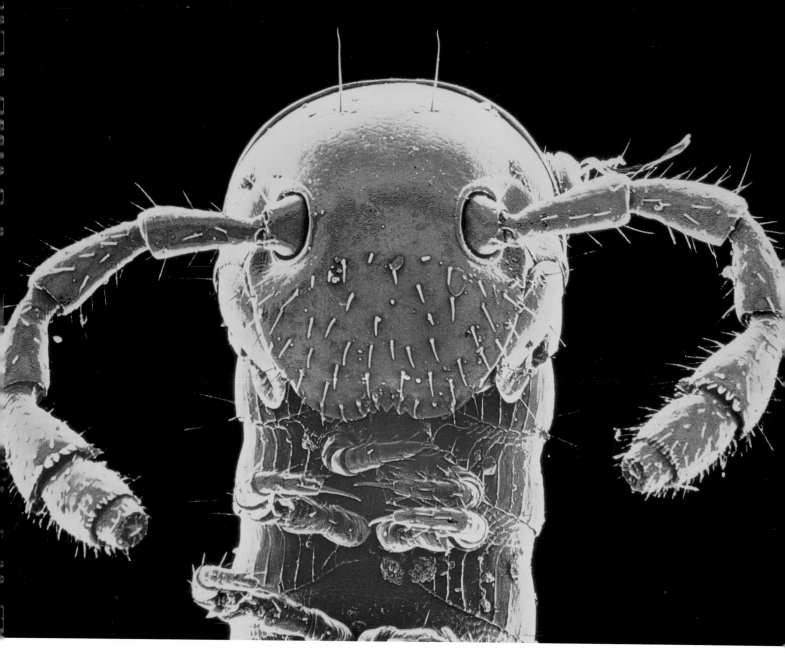

Particles of soil then stick to the eggs making them difficult to see. Some centipede species hide the eggs in the soil or under decaying leaves. Other centipedes put bundles of eggs in small nests and coil around them until they hatch.

The word 'millipede' means 1,000 feet, but the ones in our gardens have no more than 200. Millipedes don't hunt animals, they mostly eat plants. Like centipedes they live in soil and under old leaves.

A colour-enhanced picture of a millipede head, highly magnified.

Most millipedes build simple nests for their eggs. The young emerge with just three pairs of legs and within hours they shed their outer skin to reveal four pairs of legs. They will shed their skins six times over the next few months, gaining more segments and legs. The millipede is defenceless until the new covering of skin has grown, but most species build a nest and stay inside until the new covering is hard.

Early birds

Perhaps the most familiar, and most adaptable, town birds are house sparrows. They have followed humans into the coldest cities of northern Sweden, and the steamy tropical towns in central Brazil. They have even been found happily living and breeding down coal mines.

Each sparrow eats about 4 kg of food in a year – mostly grains, but also the scraps of food it can find in streets. Its stout beak is perfectly suited to this kind of food. Sparrows breed in colonies, building rather untidy nests behind gutters and in roofs, which are a warmer and drier places than trees. They even use paper and other litter to build their nests, so are perfectly adapted to all aspects of town life.

Many birds will visit gardens for food each day. Few will nest in gardens since there are usually not many trees and shrubs for them. If you ever see birds nesting, never try to investigate the eggs. Pulling branches aside to get a better look can damage the nest, and parents will desert a nest if they see it has been interfered with.

The blackbird is another very familiar garden visitor. It is intelligent with little fear of humans, and with very good hearing. When you see a blackbird standing still with its head cocked to one side, it is listening to the sound of worms just beneath the surface of the soil. The blackbird has a long beak ideal for eating its varied diet – from worms and insects to fruit.

Crimson rosellas in an Australian garden.

An American robin — common in the USA and Canada.

A blackbird searching for insects and worms.

MAKE A BIRD TABLE

Begin with a wooden tray about 0·5 m by 0·5 m. Fix four pieces of wood (each about 3 cm high) around the edges to make a rim – but leave gaps in the corners for rain to run off. With an adult to help you, nail or screw the tray to a 2 m long wooden post. Dig a hole in the ground and plant the post so the tray is about 1·5 m high.

Make sure you position the bird table away from bushes or walls where a cat can reach it, and where you can also see it from a window.

Leave out kitchen scraps and breadcrumbs all year except in the summer. Always have a shallow dish of water for birds to drink from and bathe in.

Bird table.

bread

water

bird seed

fruit

bacon rind

coconut

peanuts

Top dogs

Creatures as different as the opossum, racoon and red fox have each adapted to cities in a similar way. They all live in the same way in cities in different countries.

In many European and some North American cities the red fox is a permanent resident, making its den in parks and gardens. In North America, the racoon shares living space with the fox, and in Australia and New Zealand the opossums invade towns in large numbers, often living in the roofs of houses. All these animals are very different, but they have adapted to the town environment in the same way. They eat a huge variety of foods and hunt small animals, eat litter in streets and scavenge in dustbins.

These animals are at the top of the food chain. They have fewer natural enemies in town, and it is easier for them to find food. There are many quiet places in gardens and parks for foxes to set up home and give birth to young. People think these animals live only by scavenging. In fact, just one-third of a town fox's food is scavenged. Wild birds and mammals, insects, earthworms and the occasional pet cat make up most of the rest of its diet.

▲ Brushtail possum sometimes found in Australian gardens and roofs.

◄ The beautiful racoon is an expert climber.

Suburban habitat for a fox.

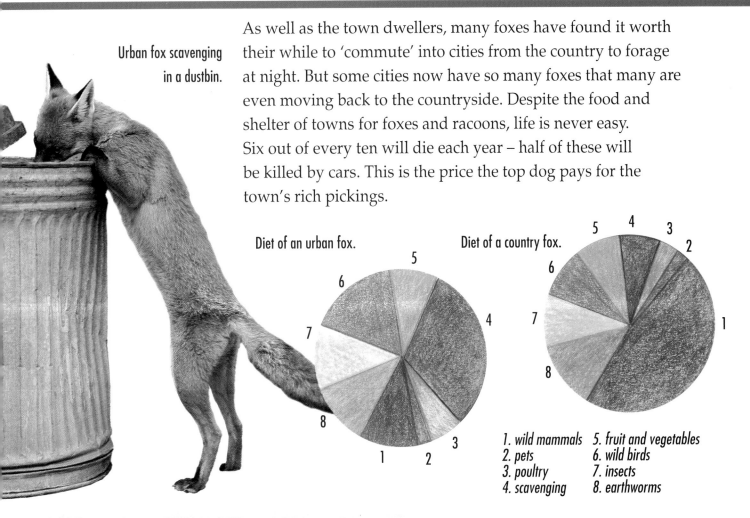

Urban fox scavenging in a dustbin.

As well as the town dwellers, many foxes have found it worth their while to 'commute' into cities from the country to forage at night. But some cities now have so many foxes that many are even moving back to the countryside. Despite the food and shelter of towns for foxes and racoons, life is never easy. Six out of every ten will die each year – half of these will be killed by cars. This is the price the top dog pays for the town's rich pickings.

Diet of an urban fox.

Diet of a country fox.

1. wild mammals
2. pets
3. poultry
4. scavenging
5. fruit and vegetables
6. wild birds
7. insects
8. earthworms

Only about one-third of a town fox's diet is scavenged – and inner city foxes scavenge the most. They will raid food from bird tables and dustbins but will find fewer earthworms, wild animals and pets than suburban foxes. In autumn, town foxes rely a lot on fruit and vegetables.

DID YOU KNOW?

Cry wolf

In the summer of 1993, the Russian city of Khabarovsk was invaded. Wolves were coming into the city and taking so many chickens and other livestock from people that city officials put a price on the heads of the wolves. Anyone who killed a wolf would receive a prize of 10,000 roubles (US $15) – about one-third of a monthly wage. Wolves in towns is not a new problem. In New York 200 years ago city officials paid a bounty for each wolf killed by a resident.

Snakes to monkeys!

In quiet and undisturbed gardens, a snake might be found sunning itself. Up to a metre or more in length, the grass snake in the UK is an excellent swimmer and feeds mostly on frogs and toads. Although it is not poisonous, it can give out a bad-smelling slime if angry or attacked. Poisonous snakes such as the rattlesnake in the south-west USA are far more dangerous, but fortunately are not frequent visitors to towns.

You may, however, still meet a slowworm slithering from under a rock after a rain storm. This is not a snake, nor is it a worm! It is a legless lizard which feeds on slugs. It is rather slow, but has a clever way of escaping if attacked: it can make its tail snap off, which then wriggles around attracting the attention of the attacker while the slow worm slowly makes its escape.

A gecko on mosquito netting. The sticky pads on their toes allow geckos to run across ceilings after insects.

The adder is the UK's most common snake. It likes quiet places and will find spots to sun itself.

In cities in warm climates other lizards, the geckos, are welcome guests. In India especially, these fat, large-headed creatures catch and eat many insects. They may even be taught to come to the dining table for scraps of food! In Bangkok, it is believed to be a sign of good luck if a gecko cries out when a baby is born.

Almost as colourful as geckos are the vultures which gather in the suburbs of many Indian towns, providing a useful role as scavengers. Any animal remains are eaten up at high speed, rather than rot and become sources of disease in the high temperatures. Indian cities are also host to Langur monkeys. They live and play in parks and gardens, climbing trees and buildings along with another species of monkey called the macaque. More monkeys live in India's cities than in the country's forests.

Langur, or leaf, monkeys tend to spend their days in trees in India, eating fruit and leaves. Some species are believed to be sacred and are allowed to roam through towns and temples helping themselves to food.

This Agama lizard is in a Kenyan garden and is about 40 cm long.

Glossary

Adapt To change and adjust to the environment.

Bacteria Single celled living things found everywhere. Some cause disease, but others are useful, decomposing dead life forms for example.

Cells All living things are made up of cells, the smallest units of life.

Carnivore A living thing that feeds on animals.

Colonize To slowly become established in a place.

Crustaceans A group of animals including woodlice, crabs, prawns and lobsters.

Ecology The study of how living things affect each other, and how they are affected by their environment. The word was invented by the scientist, Ellen Swallow, in 1892.

Environment Everything, both living and non-living, that surrounds and affects a life form.

Food chain A chain of life forms through which energy is passed, usually because they feed on each other.

Hibernate A kind of sleep when an animal's functions slow down to survive times of cold.

Larva Some creatures such as insects undergo great changes as they grow from egg to adult. A larva emerges from an egg and sheds its skin several time to allow for growth. Grubs (for beetles), maggots (for flies) and caterpillars (for butterflies) are all larvae.

Mucus A sticky liquid given out by some animals.

Nematode Tiny, worm-like animals that are present everywhere.

Parasite A living thing which feeds on another without giving anything back in return.

Proboscis The long tube-like tongue of a butterfly or moth.

Pupa The stage in a creature's development between larva and adult.

Roost A support on which birds and bats rest and sleep.

Species The name given to the smallest grouping or 'type' of plant and animal. There are believed to be about 30 million different species on the Earth.

Viruses Tiny, basic life forms which can only reproduce inside the cell of a living thing.

Resources

Organizations to contact

United Kingdom

Bat Conservation Trust
Conservation Foundation
1 Kensington Gore
London SW7 2AR

British Trust for Conservation
Volunteers
36 St Mary's Street
Wallingford
Oxfordshire OX10 0EU

Butterfly Conservation
PO Box 222, Dedham
Essex CO7 6EY

The Fox Project
11 Caister Rd, Tonbridge
Kent TN9 1UT

Royal Society for the
Protection of Birds
The Lodge, Sandy
Bedfordshire SG19 2DL

Urban Wildlife Centre
11 Albert St
Birmingham B4 7UA

For your local Urban Wildlife Group
contact:
Royal Society for Nature Conservation
22 The Green, Nettleham
Lincoln LN2 2NR

Australia

Australian Association for
Environmental Education
GPO Box 112
Canberra
ACT 2601

Australian Conservation Foundation
340 Gore Street
Fitzroy VIC 3065

Total Environment Centre
18 Argyle Street
Sydney 2000

Canada

Canadian Museum of Nature
PO Box 3443, Station D
Ottawa K1P 6P4

International Council for Local
Environmental Initiatives
City Hall
East Tower, 8th Floor
Toronto
Ontario M5H 2N2

New Zealand

Environment and Conservation
Organizations of New Zealand
PO Box 11057
Wellington

Books to read

Chris Baines, *The Wild Side of Town*,
BBC Books, 1986

Michael Chinery, *The Living Garden*,
Dorling Kindersley, 1986

Jennifer Cochrane, *Urban Ecology*,
Wayland, 1987

Ron Freethy, *Wildlife in Towns*,
Crowood Press, 1986

Ken Hoy, *Junior Naturalist in the Town*,
Guild, 1985

Alan C Jenkins, *Wildlife in the City*,
Webb & Bower, 1982

Terry Jennings, *Small Garden Animals*,
Oxford, 1987

Dick King-Smith, *Town Watch*,
Puffin, 1987

Sally Morgan, *Life in the Cities*,
Two-Can, 1993

Wildlife on Your Doorstep,
Reader's Digest, 1986

Tony Soper, *The Bird Table Book*,
David and Charles, 1986

Ron Wilson, *The Urban Dweller's
Wildlife Companion*, Blandford, 1983

Index

Numbers in **bold** refer to an illustration; numbers in *italics* refer to a project or case study.